Bake through the Bible

at Christmas

12 fun cooking activities to explore the Christmas story with young children

Design and illustration by André Parker
Edited by Alison Mitchell

Bake through the Bible at Christmas
©Susie Bentley-Taylor and Bekah Moore/The Good Book Company, 2015

All Bible references taken from the Holy Bible, New International Version. Copyright © 1979, 1984, 2011 by Biblica. Used by permission.

Published by The Good Book Company
Tel (UK): 0333 123 0880, International: +44 (0) 208 942 0880 Email: info@thegoodbook.co.uk
UK: www.thegoodbook.co.uk   North America: www.thegoodbook.com
Australia: www.thegoodbook.com.au   New Zealand: www.thegoodbook.co.nz

Food photography by Gavin Kinnaird Food prepared by Tom Beard

Additional photography ©istockphoto.com/André Parker ISBN: 9781910307984 Printed by Proost Industries NV, Belgium

Contents

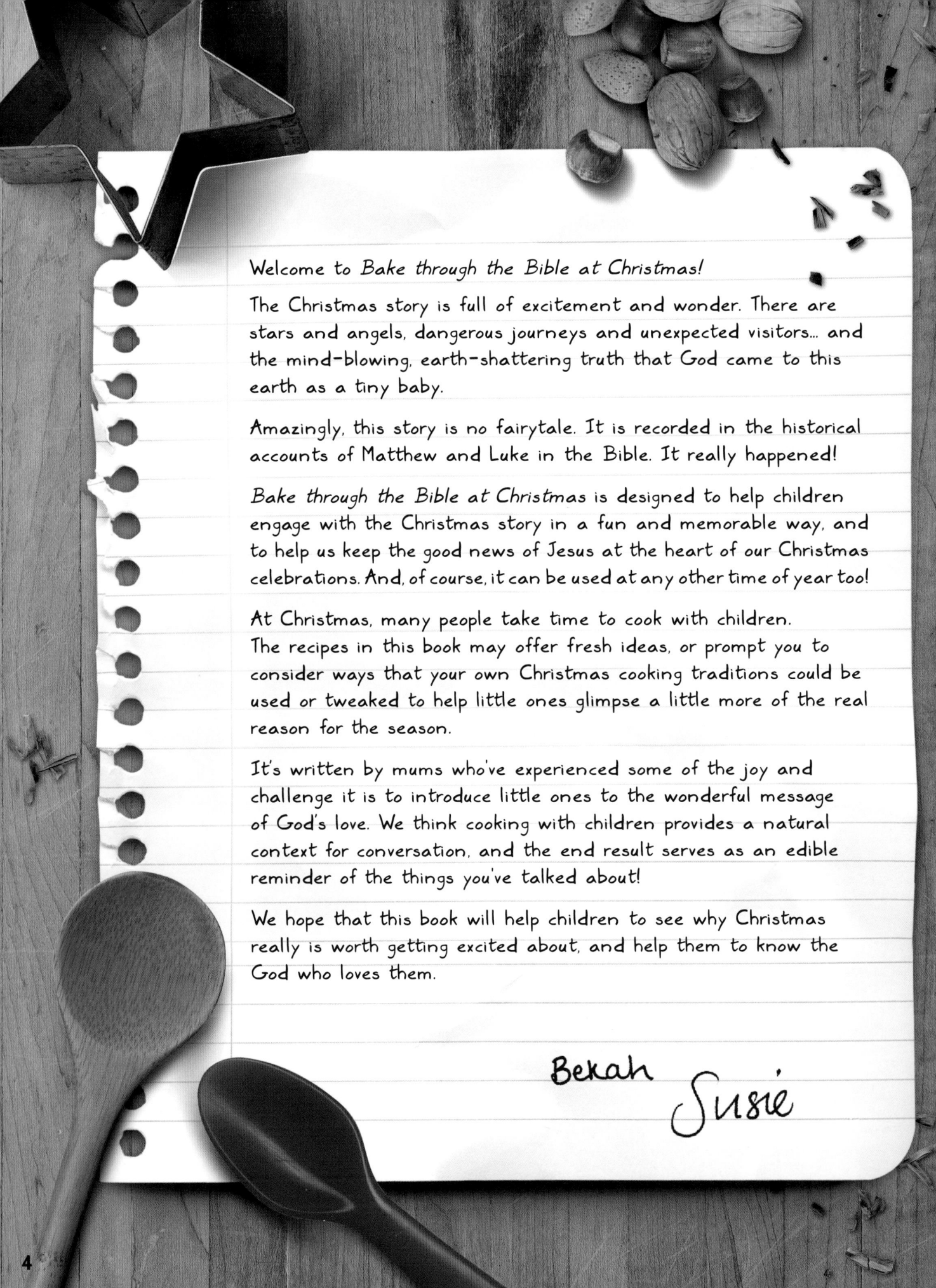

Welcome to *Bake through the Bible at Christmas!*

The Christmas story is full of excitement and wonder. There are stars and angels, dangerous journeys and unexpected visitors... and the mind-blowing, earth-shattering truth that God came to this earth as a tiny baby.

Amazingly, this story is no fairytale. It is recorded in the historical accounts of Matthew and Luke in the Bible. It really happened!

Bake through the Bible at Christmas is designed to help children engage with the Christmas story in a fun and memorable way, and to help us keep the good news of Jesus at the heart of our Christmas celebrations. And, of course, it can be used at any other time of year too!

At Christmas, many people take time to cook with children. The recipes in this book may offer fresh ideas, or prompt you to consider ways that your own Christmas cooking traditions could be used or tweaked to help little ones glimpse a little more of the real reason for the season.

It's written by mums who've experienced some of the joy and challenge it is to introduce little ones to the wonderful message of God's love. We think cooking with children provides a natural context for conversation, and the end result serves as an edible reminder of the things you've talked about!

We hope that this book will help children to see why Christmas really is worth getting excited about, and help them to know the God who loves them.

Bekah

Susie

How to use this book

Don't feel you have to be a good cook! Rather, we hope this is a way to include children in an activity that (to varying degrees) is a part of everyone's day-to-day life.

The cooking activities are designed to help unpack Bible truths for children. They are a means to an end. So it really doesn't matter if the cakes turn out a bit gooey or the gingerbread burnt round the edges. If a seed of biblical truth has been planted in a child's heart, praise God for that!

The book takes you through the events of the very first Christmas. It can be used to help children follow the biblical account of Christmas, though each activity also works well on its own.

Each unit is made up of the following:

The Bible story

A story from God's word, simply explained, for you to read with your child.

Instructions

Look out for this symbol. It shows steps that would be best done by an adult.

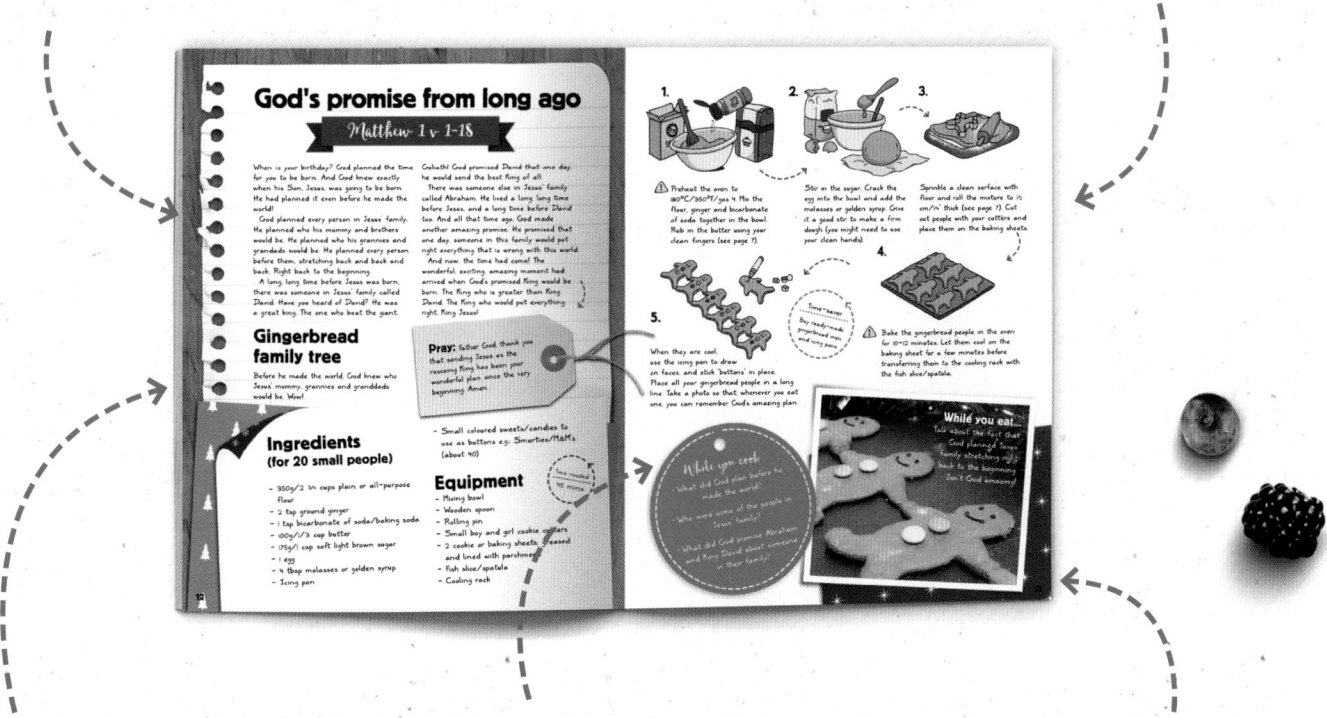

The cooking activity

This includes time-saving suggestions if you're pushed for time. See "Cooking with Children" on page 6 for more ideas.

While you cook

Questions to help your child understand the story. You may want to read the story and talk these through before beginning to cook—or you may choose to discuss them as you cook.

While you eat

A question to discuss once the cooking is done and the product finished. Your child might also like to use what they've cooked to tell someone else about the Bible story.

Cooking with children

Many children enjoy cooking from a very young age. It has numerous educational benefits: it encourages communication, develops motor skills and gives opportunity to practise listening skills and following instructions. Nevertheless, it can be a daunting prospect. Some parents feel they aren't very competent themselves in the kitchen, while others feel their children have too short a concentration span for any kind of cooking to take place successfully.

We want to assure you that cooking is possible for everyone! Some children will help their parents with a recipe from start to finish. Others will help mix the ingredients for a few seconds before getting distracted, and then return later to lick the bowl clean.

The level of participation doesn't really matter. If your child has enjoyed the experience, you can consider it worthwhile. And you might find you quite enjoy it yourself!

We want the cooking activities to help reinforce the wonderful truths of the Bible. So if you can find just one way to involve your child with the baking—and then use the finished product to talk about the Bible truth it goes with—what a success! If your hidden surprise cake is burnt, your gingerbread manger crooked or your pyramid toast falls over—and yet you've both had fun and you've been able to share how wonderful God is with your child—what a success!

We hope the following tips will encourage you to bake through the Bible this Christmas.

Prepare your recipe

Look at the recipe and any time-saving tips, and decide how much you'd like to do.

Decide which steps your child will help you with, and which you'll do before you call your child in to help you.

Work out when it will be best to do your recipe. Some recipes can be done in two parts, sometimes over two days.

Prepare your ingredients

You may want to involve your child in checking which ingredients you don't have and shopping for them. The shopping lists for each recipe are available to download—see page 48 for web details.

Decide whether your child can help you weigh out/cut the ingredients or if you should do it before they come in to help.

Prepare your kitchen

Move anything dangerous out of your child's reach. Also, look out for the "warning" symbol ⚠ used in some recipes to show steps that would be best done by an adult.

Find an apron or old clothes for your child.

Consider sitting at the table, maybe with your child fastened in a booster seat, to encourage them to sit still.

As well as the equipment listed for each recipe, consider buying a small rolling pin (large ones can be dangerous if dropped or thrown), reusable non-stick lining parchment (to save time greasing and lining tins), and a portable timer (so your gingerbread won't burn while you're upstairs putting the washing away).

Be prepared for lots of mess. That way, you won't be frustrated when that bowl of flour falls onto the floor!

Baking tips

Rubbing in butter (p9, 13, 25)

Your hands need to be clean and cold. Use the ends of your fingers to squash the butter. Every few seconds, use your whole hand to mix everything in the bowl together. Then get squashing with your finger tips again! Keep squashing and mixing until all the lumps of butter have gone and the mix is fine like sand.

Rolling out dough (p9, 13, 25, 26)

The dough and your hands need to be cold. Sprinkle a clean surface and your rolling pin with a little bit of flour. Put the dough in the middle of the surface and roll it from the middle to the sides. Turn the dough around and roll again. Keep going until it is even and thin enough. If the rolling pin begins to stick to the dough, sprinkle on more flour. Don't flip the dough over—keep the top as the top!

The light in the darkness

Isaiah 9 v2-7

When it's dark all around and you can't see, what do you need? A light of course!

Living without God as your friend is like living in the dark. And that is what it was like for God's people living long, long ago. They didn't love God. Their lives were dark and sad. They needed a rescue. They needed a light.

God knew what his people needed. He had already made a plan. A plan to send a light into the darkness. Not a light like a torch or a lamp. No—much better than that. The light God would send was a person!

This person would rescue God's people from the darkness.

This person would bring joy and happiness.

This person would be born as a baby, and would be called Mighty God.

He would be God's King for ever and ever.

Can you guess who God's light is?

Jesus!

Jesus, the light of the world. Promised by God a VERY long time before he was born!

Spiced star tree decorations

When your Christmas tree lights shine through these dark biscuits, you can remember that Jesus is the light in our dark world. How exciting!

Pray: Father God, thank you for Jesus, the light of the world. Thank you for your wonderful promise to send a rescuing King. Amen.

Time needed 45 mins

Ingredients
(for 12 stars)

- 150g/1 ¼ cups plain or all-purpose flour
- Pinch of salt
- Pinch of ground black pepper
- ½ tsp baking powder
- ½ tsp ground cinnamon
- Pinch of ground cloves
- 50g/¼ cup soft butter
- 50g/¼ cup soft dark brown sugar
- 1 egg, beaten
- 2 tbsp honey
- 12 boiled sweets/hard candies (ideally a little smaller than the bottle top), various colours (such as Barley Sugars, Jargonelle Pears or Sherbet Lemons)

1.

 Preheat the oven to 160°C/310°F/gas 3. Mix the flour, salt, pepper, baking powder, cinnamon and cloves together in the bowl using the wooden spoon. Rub in the butter using your clean fingers (see page 7).

Equipment

- Mixing bowl
- Wooden spoon
- Rolling pin
- Star cookie cutter
- 2 cookie or baking sheets, greased and lined with parchment

- Plastic bottle top (just smaller than the centre of your star cutter)
- Cocktail stick or toothpick
- 12 pieces of ribbon or string 20cm/8" long

2.

Stir in the sugar. Crack the egg into the bowl and add the honey. Give it a good stir to make a firm dough (you might need to use your clean hands to bring it together).

3.

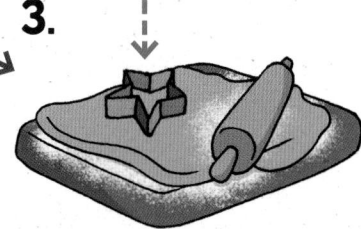

Sprinkle a clean surface with flour and roll the mixture out with the rolling pin until it is ½ cm/¼" thick (see page 7). Cut out stars and place them on the baking sheets.

Note:

The melted sweet/candy will set very hard, so be careful this doesn't become a choking hazard (or a danger to teeth) if eaten by young children.

While you cook...
- What did God's people need?
- Why?
- Who is God's light?
- What are some of the things Jesus would do?

4.

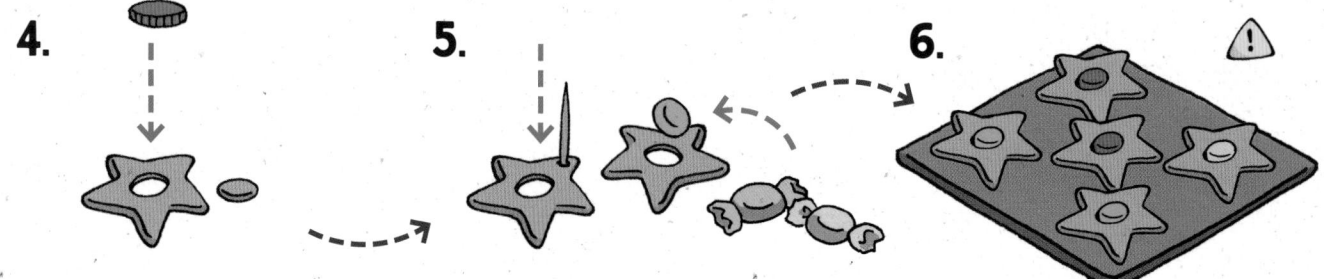

Use the bottle top to cut a hole in the middle of each star. Put the sweets in the holes.

5.

Use the toothpick or cocktail stick to make a hole (about the size of the end of a pen) in each star, at the end of one of the star's points (you will thread ribbon through this hole!).

6.

Put the stars in the oven for 18-20 minutes. (They will look very dark because they need to be well cooked and hard in order to hang on the tree.) Leave them on the trays to cool.

Note:

The biscuits will go stale very quickly on your Christmas tree, so why not keep most of them in a tin or airtight container, and hang just a few biscuits on the tree at a time.

7.

When the stars are cold, thread ribbon through each one so that you can hang them on your Christmas tree. Can you see the tree lights through the dark biscuits to remember that Jesus came as a light into our dark world?

While you eat...

Can you describe God's
light, Jesus?

God's promise from long ago

Matthew 1 v 1-18

When is your birthday? God planned the time for you to be born. And God knew exactly when his Son, Jesus, was going to be born. He had planned it even before he made the world!

God planned every person in Jesus' family. He planned who his mummy and brothers would be. He planned who his grannies and grandads would be. He planned every person before them, stretching back and back and back. Right back to the beginning.

A long, long time before Jesus was born, there was someone in Jesus' family called David. Have you heard of David? He was a great king. The one who beat the giant, Goliath! God promised David that one day, he would send the best King of all.

There was someone else in Jesus' family called Abraham. He lived a long, long time before Jesus, and a long time before David too. And all that time ago, God made another amazing promise. He promised that one day, someone in this family would put right everything that is wrong with this world.

And now, the time had come! The wonderful, exciting, amazing moment had arrived when God's promised King would be born. The King who is greater than King David. The King who would put everything right. King Jesus!

Gingerbread family tree

Before he made the world, God knew who Jesus' mummy, grannies and granddads would be. Wow!

Pray: Father God, thank you that sending Jesus as the rescuing King has been your wonderful plan since the very beginning. Amen.

Ingredients
(for 20 small people)

- 350g/2 ¾ cups plain or all-purpose flour
- 2 tsp ground ginger
- 1 tsp bicarbonate of soda/baking soda
- 100g/½ cup butter
- 175g/⅘ cup soft light brown sugar
- 1 egg
- 4 tbsp molasses or golden syrup
- Icing pen
- Small coloured sweets/candies to use as buttons e.g. Smarties/M&M's (about 40)

Equipment

- Mixing bowl
- Wooden spoon
- Rolling pin
- Small boy and girl cookie cutters
- 2 cookie or baking sheets, greased and lined with parchment
- Fish slice/spatula
- Cooling rack

Time needed 45 mins

1.

Preheat the oven to 180°C/350°F/gas 4. Mix the flour, ginger and bicarbonate of soda together in the bowl. Rub in the butter using your clean fingers (see page 7).

2.

Stir in the sugar. Crack the egg into the bowl and add the molasses or golden syrup. Give it a good stir to make a firm dough (you might need to use your clean hands).

3.

Sprinkle a clean surface with flour and roll the mixture to ½ cm/¼" thick (see page 7). Cut out people with your cutters and place them on the baking sheets.

4.

Bake the gingerbread people in the oven for 10-12 minutes. Let them cool on the baking sheet for a few minutes before transferring them to the cooling rack with the fish slice/spatula.

5.

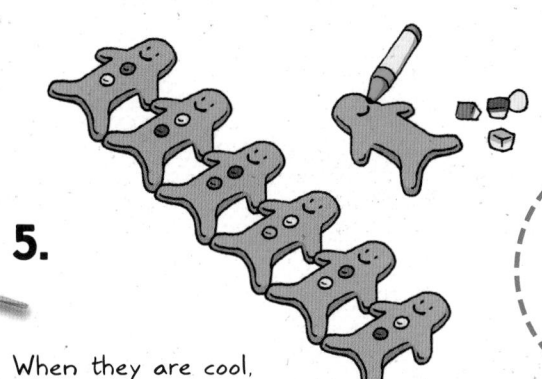

When they are cool, use the icing pen to draw on faces, and stick 'buttons' in place. Place all your gingerbread people in a long line. Take a photo so that, whenever you eat one, you can remember God's amazing plan.

Time-saver

Buy ready-made gingerbread men and icing pens

While you cook...

- What did God plan before he made the world?

- Who were some of the people in Jesus' family?

- What did God promise Abraham and King David about someone in their family?

While you eat...

Talk about the fact that God planned Jesus' family stretching right back to the beginning. Isn't God amazing!

An angel's message for Mary

Luke 1 v 26-38

Mary was an ordinary woman. She lived an ordinary life in an ordinary little town. But one day, something not very ordinary happened. Something quite extraordinary. An angel came to bring her a message from God. An angel! With a message from God!

Mary was scared. "Don't be afraid, Mary," said the angel. "God has chosen you for something special. You are going to have a baby and you are to call him Jesus. He will be great. He will be God's own Son. He will be King for ever and ever."

"How can this happen?" asked Mary.

"God will make it happen by his Spirit," the angel replied.

"I want to please God," Mary said.

God's own Son would grow as a tiny baby inside Mary. What a special, special baby Jesus would be.

Pray: Thank you God, you sent your Son, Jesus, into this world to be King for ever. Help us to understand how amazing that is. Amen.

Cranberry angel cakes

An angel brought a very special message to Mary.

Ingredients (for 12 cakes)

For the cakes:
- 50g/¼ cup butter, cubed
- 225ml/8 fl oz milk
- 300g/2 ½ cups plain or all-purpose flour
- 2 tsp baking powder
- 1 tsp mixed spice or pumpkin pie spice (optional)
- 150g/¾ cup caster or superfine granulated sugar
- 100g/½ cup dried cranberries
- 1 egg

For the buttercream/frosting:
- 100g/2/3 cup butter, softened
- 200g/1 ½ cups icing sugar/powdered sugar
- ½ tsp vanilla essence
- 12 white chocolate buttons
- Edible glitter or sprinkles

1.

- Small saucepan
- 2 mixing bowls
- Wooden spoon
- Standard 12-hole muffin pan or tin with cases
- Cooling rack
- Sieve
- Sharp knife

Time needed
60 mins

⚠ Preheat the oven to 200°C/400°F/gas 6. Put the butter and milk into the pan. Put it onto a low heat until the butter melts; then let it cool for 5 minutes.

2.

Sift the flour, baking powder and mixed spice into the mixing bowl. Stir in the sugar and cranberries.

3.

Break the egg into the mixing bowl, add the milk and butter, and stir until it is all just combined. Then spoon the mixture into the muffin cases.

While you cook...

- Who did God send with a message for Mary?
- What did the angel say to Mary?
- How did Mary feel?
- What was so special about Mary's son?

4.

Put the cupcakes into the oven for 15 minutes. Then put them on a wire rack to cool for about an hour.

5.

To make the buttercream/frosting, sift the icing sugar into a large bowl. Add the butter and beat together until smooth. Stir in the vanilla essence.

6.

When the cakes are cool, use a sharp knife to cut a circle from the middle of each one (about 5cm/2" wide and deep). Cut each circle in half to make two wings.

Time-saver

Buy ready-made muffins and buttercream/frosting, then follow steps 6 and 7

7.

Fill the holes with the buttercream or frosting, and put the wings on either side of the icing. Put a chocolate button at one end of the icing for the angel's head. Pour glitter or sprinkles in a line for the angel's body.

While you eat...

Give an angel cake to
the person who helped you
bake and tell them what
the angel said to Mary.

Elizabeth's "impossible" baby

Luke 1 v 36-45

Can you touch your ear with your elbow? Or your eye with your tongue? No! Impossible!

Elizabeth was very old. So was her husband, Zechariah. They thought that they were too old to have a baby. Far too old! Impossible!

But nothing is impossible for God. God can do amazing things. And so, guess what? God gave Elizabeth and Zechariah a baby. The baby started to grow inside Elizabeth. 'This is God's work,' said Elizabeth. 'God has been so kind to me.'

Mary went to visit Elizabeth. They were both so excited about what God was doing. Elizabeth's baby jumped for joy inside her!

Elizabeth was old. But she had a baby growing inside her. Mary didn't have a husband. But she had a baby growing inside her. Mary had God's Forever-King, Jesus, growing inside her!

Impossible? Not for God. Nothing is impossible with God.

Hidden surprise cake

Elizabeth had a baby in her tummy. She thought that would be impossible! But all things are possible for God.

Pray: Thank you God that nothing is impossible for you. You even sent your Forever-King into our world. Help me to trust you more and more. Amen.

Ingredients
(for 1 loaf cake/8 servings)

For the cake:
- 1 large, light-coloured rectangular cake (e.g. Madeira cake)
- 4 eggs
- 140g/2/3 cup caster or superfine granulated sugar
- 120g/1 cup self-raising flour
- 35g/1/3 cup cocoa powder

For the icing:
- 55g/1/4 cup butter, softened
- 25g/1/5 cup cocoa powder
- 90g/3/4 cup icing sugar/ powdered sugar
- White icing pen/white chocolate icing tube
- Christmas cake decorations or sprinkles

Time needed
1 1/2 hours
(plus 1 1/2hrs to cool and to set)

Equipment

- Large sharp knife
- Small boy cookie cutter
- 2 mixing bowls
- Electric or hand whisk
- Large metal spoon
- Loaf tin, greased and lined with parchment
- Bread or chopping board
- Sieve
- Wooden spoon
- Table/eating knife

2.

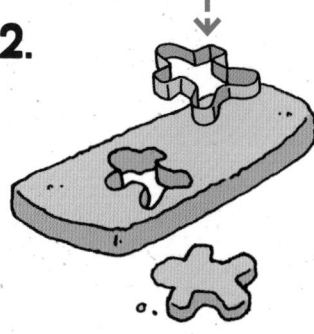

Use your cutter to cut out as many 'boys' from the cake as you can.

1.

Preheat the oven to 170°C/325°F/gas 3. Slice the cake into three, lengthways, to make three long and thin rectangles.

3.

Break the eggs into the mixing bowl. Add the sugar and whisk for 5 minutes until the mixture is thick and almost white. Gently fold in the flour and cocoa powder using the big metal spoon.

4.

Stand the 'boys' in the loaf tin tightly in front of each other, with no gaps between them. Carefully pour in some mixture at either end of the tin, then at the sides, then on top of the 'boys'.

While you cook...

- What did Elizabeth think was impossible? Why?

- How was God kind to Elizabeth?

- What impossible thing did God do for Mary?

- Is anything impossible for God?

Time-saver

Buy a ready-made gingerbread man and hide it in a bowl underneath yogurt.

5.

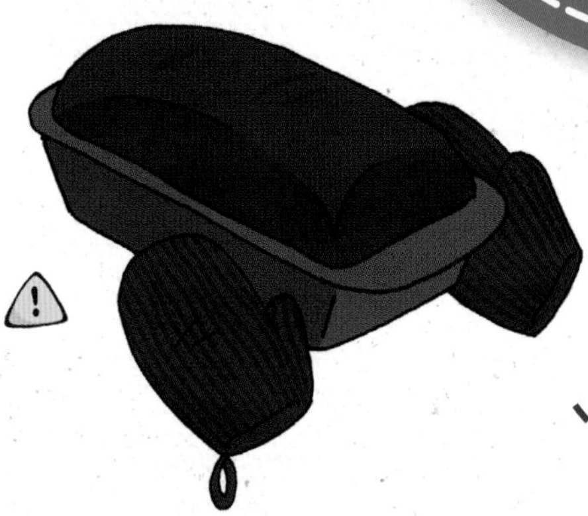

Put the cake in the oven for 40 minutes, until it is springy when you gently push a finger in. Leave to cool in the tin for about an hour, before turning out onto the board.

6.

To make the icing, sieve the icing sugar and cocoa powder into the mixing bowl. Add the butter and mix with the wooden spoon until the icing is smooth.

7.

Use the knife to spread the icing on the top of the cake. Decorate with your Christmas cake decorations or with sprinkles. Leave to set for 30 minutes.

While you eat...

Take the whole cake to someone who hasn't seen you make it. As an adult cuts it open (straight down, in the middle), look at the surprise on their face! Can you explain to them why Elizabeth was surprised too?

An angel's message for Joseph

Matthew 1 v 18-25

Joseph loved Mary. But they weren't married yet. So when Mary told Joseph that she was going to have a baby, Joseph was puzzled. He thought that he should say goodbye to Mary. He thought that they should end their plan to get married. He thought that they shouldn't see each other again.

But God had a different plan. He sent an angel to speak to Joseph. The angel had a special message. The angel said: "Joseph! Don't be afraid. You can still marry Mary. She will have a baby boy. He is God's Son. You must call him Jesus! Because Jesus means 'He will save his people from their sins'."

This baby—this Jesus—would save people. He would rescue people. Rescue people from being God's enemies and facing his punishment. Rescue people so that we can enjoy being friends with God for ever. What an amazing message.

So Joseph married Mary. The special baby was born. And Joseph gave him the name Jesus.

Jesus! God saves.

Do you know what your name means? God's King is called Jesus because Jesus means "the one who saves". And that is exactly what Jesus does!

Fruity yogurt pancakes

Jesus' name is very important. It means he is the promised Rescuer!

Pray: Thank you God that you sent Jesus to rescue us. Thank you that we can be your friends for ever. Amen.

Ingredients
(for 8 pancakes)

- 150g/1 1/4 cups plain or all-purpose flour
- Pinch of salt
- 2 tsp baking powder
- 2 tbsp caster or fine granulated sugar
- 1 egg, beaten
- 150ml/2/3 cup natural or Greek yogurt
- 50ml/2 fl oz milk
- 1 tbsp oil
- Fruit, to serve

Equipment

- Sieve
- Mixing bowl
- Wooden spoon
- Frying pan
- Small polythene/freezer/ sandwich - bag
- Scissors
- Spatula

Time needed
20 mins

Time-saver
Buy pancakes and draw a 'J' on them with icing pens

1.

Sift the flour, salt, baking powder and sugar into the bowl. Then use the spoon to make a hole in the middle of the mixture.

2.

Pour the beaten egg, yogurt and milk into the hole and mix until just smooth.

3.

Heat the oil in the frying pan over a medium heat for a few seconds. Then take the pan off the heat.

6.

Serve the pancake with your fruit.

5.

Put the pan back on the heat and cook the pancake for about 1 ½ minutes. Then use the spatula to flip it over and cook the other side for another 1 ½ minutes. Put the pancake on a plate; then cook the other 7 pancakes.

4.

Put the pancake mixture into the polythene bag. Cut off a corner (the hole should be just big enough for an adult finger to fit in). Twist the top of the bag and use it like a pen to draw a "J" in the frying pan.

Note:

These pancakes are thick so do check that the middle is cooked, and not still raw, by cutting a hole halfway down.

While you cook...

- Why was Joseph sad?

- What did the angel tell Joseph to do?

- What does Jesus' name mean?

- What does Jesus do?

While you eat...
Why is the birth of Jesus such good news?.

Jesus is born in Bethlehem

Luke 2 v 1-7

Some stories are just made-up stories about made-up people. But not this one (or any of the stories in this book). This is a true story. A story about real people and real places. A wonderful, amazing story that really happened. Are you ready?

Far, far away, there was a little town called Bethlehem. It wasn't a big place. It wasn't an important place. But it was a very busy place. It was full of people!

That was because of a man called Caesar Augustus. He was a ruler. Everyone had to do what he said. And one day, he told everyone to go back to the town where they were born. So, little Bethlehem was full of people who had been born there.

One of those people was Joseph. He went to Bethlehem with Mary. The baby inside Mary had been growing and growing. It was almost time for the baby to be born. Quick! They needed somewhere to stay.

Knock, knock. No room! Try next door! Knock, knock. No room! Try over there! Knock, knock. No room, no room, no room…

And then it happened. It really happened. At a real time and in a real place, God's King was born into this world. God's King Jesus came as a baby! And where could Mary put him? Not in a prince's cot in a palace. Not even in a bed. No. Mary laid this most precious baby in a manger.

Gingerbread manger

This gingerbread manger will remind us that King Jesus was born in Bethlehem and placed in a manger.

Pray: Thank you God that your King, Jesus, really came into our world. Help us to trust in him and praise him. Amen.

Ingredients

- 175g/1 ½ cups plain or all-purpose flour
- 1 tsp ground ginger
- ½ tsp bicarbonate of soda/baking soda
- 50g/¼ cup butter
- 85g/⅕ cup soft light brown sugar
- 1 egg
- 2 tbsp molasses or golden syrup
- bran or crushed Shredded Wheat
- 5 jelly sweets (e.g. fruit pastilles)
- 4 giant jelly sweets/gumdrops or marshmallows
- 1 long, flat sweet (sugar belt)
- 1 tube writing icing (any colour)

Equipment

- Mixing bowl
- Wooden spoon
- Fork
- Cup
- Rolling pin
- 2 pieces of baking paper or parchment
- Sharp knife
- Manger template (see page 48)
- 1 cookie or baking sheet

Time needed 45 mins

1.

Preheat the oven to 180°C/350°F/gas 4. Mix the flour, ginger and bicarbonate of soda together in the bowl. Then rub in the butter using your clean fingers (see page 7).

2.

Stir in the sugar. Then crack the egg into the cup, mix gently with the fork and pour half into the mixing bowl. Add the molasses or golden syrup. Give it a good stir to make a firm dough (you might need to use your clean hands).

3.

Put the dough between two sheets of baking paper and roll to 5mm/ 1/4" thick (see page 7). Remove the top sheet of paper. Place the template on top of the dough and cut out the two manger pieces.

6.

For baby Jesus, stick 3 smaller jelly sweets together using the icing pen; then place him in the manger. For Mary and Joseph, stick 2 large sweets together, then a smaller one for the head. Cut the flat sweet down to make the hair/scarf and stick in place.

5.

When the pieces are cool, slot them together to make your manger. Put the bran or crushed Shredded Wheat in and around the manger for the hay.

4.

Slide the baking paper and dough pieces onto the baking tray. Put in the oven for 12-14 minutes. Leave them on the paper sheet for two minutes. Then place the template on top of each piece and cut out the middle slot.

While you cook...
- Why did Joseph and Mary go to Bethlehem?
- What was special about Mary's baby?
- Where do kings normally sleep?
- Where did the baby King Jesus sleep?

While you eat...

Can you retell the true story of when King Jesus was born?

Gingerbread nativity set

Ingredients

- 500g/4 cups plain or all-purpose flour
- 1 ½ tsp bicarbonate of soda
- 3 tsp ground ginger
- 190g/⁴/₅ cup unsalted butter
- 155g/¾ cup dark muscovado or molasses sugar
- 5 tbsp golden syrup or molasses
- 2 packets powdered egg white* (each substituting 1 egg white)
- 500g/4 cups icing sugar
- 20g/3 tbsp cocoa
- 4 jelly sweets (e.g. fruit pastilles)
- 4 smaller jelly sweets (e.g. midget gems)
- 1 long, flat sweet (sugar belt)
- Shredded Wheat or bran, crushed

*Safer than using raw eggs

Time needed
1½ hours plus setting overnight; then 1 hour plus 4 hours to finish setting

Nativity set

If you have some extra time over Christmas, here's a full nativity set to make in place of the gingerbread manger.

Equipment

- Templates (see page 48)
- 2 large mixing bowls
- Wooden spoon
- Saucepan
- Baking paper or parchment
- Rolling pin
- Table or eating knife
- Cookie or baking sheets
- Sharp knife
- Sieve
- Piping bag and nozzle with large hole
- 1 board, tray or very flat plate
- Rectangular box (15x10cm/6x4") — a 6-egg box should be perfect

Note: We have only listed basic steps here - for a more detailed set of instructions, see the download (p48)

1.

⚠️ Preheat the oven to 180°C/350°F/gas 4. Mix the flour, soda and ginger in the mixing bowl. Tip the butter, sugar and syrup into the saucepan and heat gently.

2.

Once melted, pour the mix into the bowl. Mix everything together until you have a tough dough (add a drop of water if needed).

3.

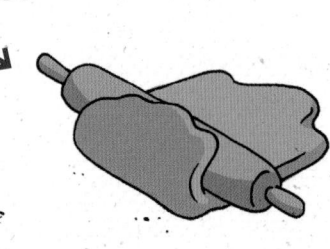

Put a large piece of baking paper onto a flat surface. Sprinkle flour onto the rolling pin and roll out the mixture until it is 5mm/¼" thick (see page 7). (You may need to do this in two halves.)

4.

Cut around the two roof templates, 2 sides and 2 manger pieces. Slide the baking paper and dough pieces onto the baking trays.

5.

Bake the pieces for 12 minutes for golden syrup or 14 minutes for molasses. The pieces should be dark and crisp. Once cool, trim the edges with the sharp knife to make them neat and crisp.

6.

Make up one egg white according to the packet's instructions. Sieve 250g/2 cups icing sugar and 10g/1 ½ tbsp cocoa into the 2nd bowl, pour in the egg white and mix well. Scrape into the piping bag.

9.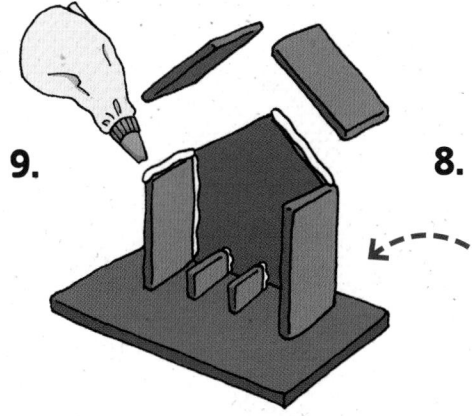

Pipe icing along the top edges of the walls and put the roof in place. Leave for at least 4 hours to dry completely.

8.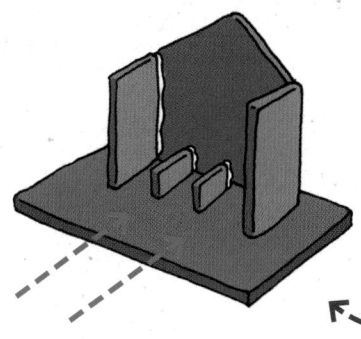

Remove the box and stick the manger in place using more icing.

7.

Use the icing to assemble the back and side pieces. Place the box between the pieces and leave overnight to dry.

10.

Use the sweets to make Mary, Joseph and baby Jesus. One the building is dry, put the bran or crushed Shredded Wheat around the floor for the hay.

The good news of Jesus' birth

Luke 2 v 8-14

It was night. It was dark. In the fields around Bethlehem there were sheep. Lots of sheep. And there were shepherds, looking after them. Maybe the shepherds were tired. Maybe they were cold. Maybe they thought it was going to be just another ordinary night. And then suddenly…

FLASH! An angel appeared. An angel! The shepherds were very frightened.

"Don't be afraid!" the angel said. "I come with wonderful news! Wonderful news for everyone! Today, in Bethlehem, God's Rescuer has been born. He is God's Forever-King. Go and see him! You will find him lying in a manger."

And then, FLASH! The sky was full—full of angels. Angels and more angels and more angels! They were so happy about God's great news. "Praise our wonderful God!" they said. "He is going to bring people into his family and fix this broken world!"

Then the angels went back to heaven. The shepherds hurried to find the special baby. What wonderful news they had heard! God's promised Rescuer had been born. The one who rescues people like us so that we can be part of God's family. Now that really is something to get excited about!

Party time!

The angels told the shepherds the most wonderful news. Let's have a party to celebrate!

Pray: Lord God, the news that King Jesus was born is the best news in the whole world! Help me to be more excited about this than anything else. Amen.

Mulled apple juice

Ingredients
(for 6 small mugs)

- 1 litre/2 pints apple juice
- 2 cinnamon sticks
- 2 cloves
- Peel from 1 orange
- "Good news!" streamer (see page 29 for instructions)

Equipment

- Large saucepan
- Wooden spoon
- Tea strainer/small sieve
- 6 mugs

Time needed
30 mins plus at least 30 mins to cool

Time-saver
Buy ready-made mulled apple juice and chocolate log. Add the streamer and iced writing to help your child celebrate the most amazing news.

1. Pour the apple juice into the pan and add the cinnamon sticks, cloves and orange peel.

2. Heat the pan on the hob/stovetop over a gentle heat for 20 minutes. Stir now and again with the wooden spoon.

3. Put the tea strainer or sieve over each mug in turn and pour the mulled apple juice in. Let it cool for at least 30 minutes.

4. Check that the juice is cool enough before serving. Then add a streamer to each mug and enjoy!

While you cook...
- Why were the shepherds frightened?
- What news did the angels give to the shepherds?
- Why were the angels so happy?
- What did the shepherds do next?

Good news streamer

Cut a small piece of wrapping paper or foil. Draw a line 2cm from one edge; then cut thin ribbons up to the line. Write "Good news!" on a separate strip of paper. Stick to the top of a straw with adhesive tape.

Ingredients
(for a log that cuts into 6 small slices)

- Small chocolate swiss roll (about 15cm/6" long)
- 40g/1/5 cup butter
- 150g/1 1/5 cups icing sugar
- 1 tbsp cocoa
- 1 tbsp milk
- Icing pen

Equipment

- Small saucepan
- Mixing bowl
- Sieve
- Wooden spoon
- Cake board or plate
- Table/eating knife

Time needed
45 mins including time to cool

Chocolate log

1.

Melt the butter in the saucepan over a low heat. Leave to cool for 10 minutes; then pour into the mixing bowl.

2.

Sieve the icing sugar and cocoa into the mixing bowl and add the milk. Mix it all together with the wooden spoon.

3.

Put the swiss roll onto the board or plate and pour the icing over it. Spread with the knife to make it smooth, if needed.

4.

Leave your chocolate log to set a little in the fridge for about 15 minutes. Then write "Jesus is born!" on the top using the icing pen. Leave the icing to set for at least 5 minutes before eating.

While you eat...

Can you explain why you are having a party? What are you celebrating?

Excited shepherds visit Jesus

Luke 2 v 15-20

What do you think shepherds do? Stand around in fields? Well, not the shepherds in this story. These shepherds were running. Running to Bethlehem.

They had just heard some amazing news. A special baby had been born there. Baby Jesus, God's promised King. An angel had told them. Now they were on their way to find this baby. No wonder they were in a hurry!

They got to Bethlehem and... there he was. Baby Jesus. They saw him with their own eyes. God's King was lying in a manger. It was just as the angel had said.

The shepherds were so excited. "Good news, everyone! Jesus is born! God's King is really here! Here to rescue us."

They just had to tell people. They wanted everyone to know. They had such wonderful news to share! Their hearts were full of thanks to God. How great, how amazing, how WONDERFUL God is!

Pray: Lord God, thank you for the wonderful news that Jesus was really born. Help me to want to share it with people I know. Amen.

Tear-and-share bread

The birth of Jesus is such good news: let's share it!

Ingredients
(for 9 portions)

- 1 garlic clove, crushed/minced
- 1 tbsp butter, fairly soft
- 1 pack ciabatta bread mix or your preferred bread mix
- 2 tbsp grated cheese

Time needed
30 mins plus 30 mins rising plus 20 mins baking

Equipment

- Large bowl
- Wooden spoon
- Electric mixer with dough hook, if you have one
- Measuring jug/cup
- Table knife
- Sharp knife
- Baking sheet, greased
- Damp cloth or oiled clingfilm/ plastic food wrap

Time-saver
Buy ready-made tear-and-share bread. Sprinkle over 2 tbsp grated cheese and warm in a hot oven for 10 minutes.

1. Mix the garlic and butter in a bowl.

2. Follow the instructions on the packet for how to mix the flour with water and knead.

3. Use your clean hands to pull the bread into a rectangle about 30cm by 20cm/12˝ by 8˝. Then spread the garlic butter all over the bread and sprinkle the cheese on top.

6. ⚠ The rolls should be much bigger and not have any gaps between them. Place in the oven for 20 minutes or until golden brown. Leave on the tray to cool.

5. Cut the bread sausage into 9 equal pieces. Place the bread pieces flat (so the swirls are facing up) and 3cm/1˝ apart on the baking sheet. Cover with a damp cloth or oiled clingfilm/plastic food wrap for 30 minutes. Preheat the oven to 200°C/400°F/gas 6.

4. Turn the bread around so that the longest side is closest to your body and hold onto it from this side. Roll the bread away from you into a long sausage.

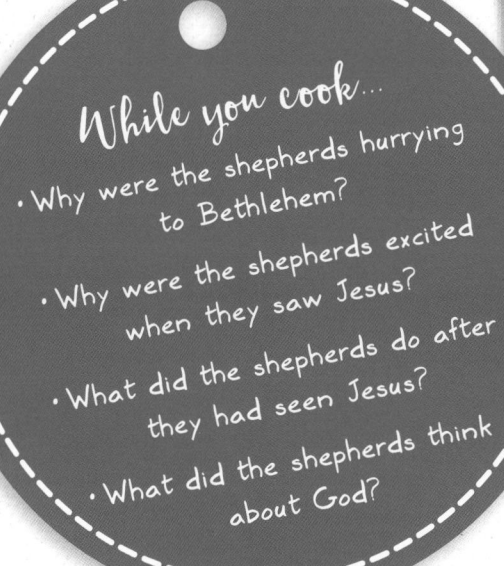

While you cook...
- Why were the shepherds hurrying to Bethlehem?
- Why were the shepherds excited when they saw Jesus?
- What did the shepherds do after they had seen Jesus?
- What did the shepherds think about God?

While you eat...
As you share the bread, think about who you could share the great news of Jesus' birth with. Could you go to church together to find out more?

Simeon and Anna meet Jesus

Luke 2 v 21-40

Baby Jesus was eight days old. Mary and Joseph took him to God's temple. They wanted to say thank you to God for this special baby.

In the temple was a man called Simeon. He loved God. God had told Simeon that he would see God's Rescuer before he died. The one God had promised long ago. Simeon had been waiting and waiting!

And then, the day came. Simeon saw Jesus come into the temple with Mary and Joseph. God showed Simeon that Jesus was the one he had been waiting for. The promised King. The promised Rescuer.

Simeon held the baby in his arms and was full of thanks to God.

"God, I see how amazing your rescue plan is!" he said. "Jesus—this little baby—is the Rescuer we've been waiting for. I've seen him! I can die a happy man!"

An old woman called Anna saw Simeon holding baby Jesus. She knew Jesus was God's Rescuer too! And so she thanked God and told everyone around her about Jesus. "Come and see! The Rescuer is here! The one who can bring people into God's own family! Hooray!"

Pray: Father in heaven, thank you for your amazing rescue plan. Thank you that because of Jesus, I can be part of your family. Amen.

Happy snowman trifle

This snowman trifle has a happy face because Simeon and Anna knew that Jesus was the Rescuer of the world and that made them VERY happy!

Ingredients

*Or substitute a large pack of vanilla or banana instant pudding

- 1 pack jelly/jello, any colour
- 1 tin of fruit or 2 handfuls of fresh fruit (NOT fresh pineapple, kiwi or papaya: these fruits will stop the jelly/jello from setting)
- 1 tin ready-made custard*
- 600ml/2 ½ cups double/heavy or whipping cream
- 1 banana
- 1 orange
- A handful of blueberries: fresh, canned or frozen (defrosted)

Equipment

- Measuring jug
- 1 large glass bowl
- Whisk
- Mixing bowl
- Wooden spoon
- Table (eating) knife
- Chopping board
- Piping bag with nozzle

Time needed
....
10 mins
plus 6 hours
setting time

1. Make up the jelly/jello according to the instructions on the packet. Place the tinned fruit or handfuls of fresh fruit into the bowl; then pour in the jelly/jello.

2. Put the bowl in the fridge to set for at least 6 hours. When the jelly/jello is set, pour the custard on top.

3. Whip the cream in the mixing bowl with a whisk. It should hold its shape for two seconds when you put a clean finger into it and make a line. Spoon the cream on top of the custard, but keep 2 spoons of cream to one side. Smooth out the cream using a spoon and table knife.

Time-saver
Use squirty cream/ Reddi wip

5. Make a smiley face with the fruit on top of the cream. Peel the orange and break off one piece. Stick the orange segment into the trifle for a nose. Use the blueberries for the eyes and smiley mouth.

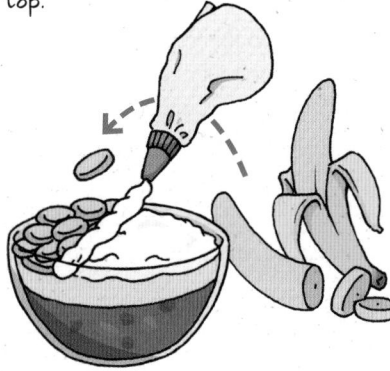

4. Make the snowman's hat. Peel the banana and slice it into thin rounds using the table knife. Put the banana pieces on top of the cream, covering a third of the bowl to make a hat. To make the hat woolly, put the remaining cream into the piping bag. Pipe along the bottom of the hat and put a big round splodge for the bobble at the top.

While you cook...
- Why did Mary and Joseph take baby Jesus to the temple?
- What did God promise to Simeon?
- What did Simeon know about Jesus?
- What did Anna do after she had seen Jesus?

While you eat...
Why were Simeon and Anna so very happy?.

The wise men find Jesus

Matthew 2 v 1-12

Far, far away from the place where Jesus was born, some wise men saw a star. A beautiful, sparkling star. A star that meant that a King had been born. A King who would be King over everyone. Even them. They wanted to see him. And so they followed the star. They followed it for a long, long time. They really wanted to find this King.
But who would it be?
The star took them all the way to a country called Israel.
But which town?
They followed the star to a little town called Bethlehem.
But which house?

The star stopped over a house. This is where they would find the King. The King they had been searching for! They were so happy.
But who would they find inside?
Jesus!
The little boy they saw was King Jesus. The King they so wanted to meet.
And so they treated him just as God's King should be treated. They got on their knees before him. They praised him. They gave him precious treasures.
They had seen God's King! Not just the king of one country. The King of the whole world!

Crown sandwiches

The wise men were so happy to find King Jesus who would be king over everyone!
Kings wear crowns, and these sandwiches are shaped like crowns, so we can remember that Jesus is the King of the whole world.

Pray: Father in heaven, thank you for sending your chosen King, Jesus. Help us to treat him as our King by loving him and giving him what we have. Amen.

Ingredients
(for 2 crown sandwiches)

- 2 slices of bread
- butter or other spread
- ingredients for your chosen filling (see opposite)

Equipment

- Bread knife
- Table or eating knife
- Vegetable grater (if making carrot sandwiches)
- Sharp knife (if making ham, cheese and pear sandwiches)

Time needed
10 mins

1.

Turkey and cranberry

Spread 2 slices of bread with butter or other spread. Spread cranberry sauce over one slice. Put pieces of turkey over the sauce.

2.

Carrot

Spread 1 slice of bread with cream cheese or soft cheese or houmous and another slice of bread with butter or other spread. Grate ½ medium carrot and put the carrot on top of the cheese.

3. ⚠️

Ham, cheese and pear

Spread 2 slices of bread with butter or other spread. Put a slice of ham on one slice of bread. Chop ½ pear thinly and put it on top of the ham. Place a slice of cheese on top of the pear. Put this slice of bread under a hot grill for 2 minutes or until the cheese melts (optional). Allow the melted cheese to cool.

Chop the crusts off the bread with the bread knife; then cut a zig-zag down the middle to make two crowns.

While you cook...
- What did the wise men see?
- What did the wise men know when they saw the star?
- How did the wise men treat Jesus?

While you eat...

What do crowns remind us about Jesus?

The escape to Egypt

Matthew 2 v 13-23

When Jesus was a little boy, an angel brought a message to Joseph. "Quick, Joseph! You and your family need to get away. Go to Egypt. King Herod wants to kill Jesus."

King Herod hated Jesus. He wanted to be the only king. He didn't want Jesus to be King.

So Joseph, Mary and Jesus left their house. They left their town. They left their country. It was a long, long journey. They went to Egypt, where they would be safe.

The angel was right. King Herod tried to find Jesus to kill him. But he couldn't find him. He had gone far, far away to the country of Egypt. God was keeping him safe.

Some time later, the angel brought another message to Joseph. "Joseph, it's safe to go back!"

So Joseph, Mary and Jesus went back. And all the time, God kept them safe. God can do anything. Of course he could keep his King safe! God has FAR more power than anyone in the whole wide world.

Pray: Father God, thank you that you looked after Jesus. Thank you that you look after us, too. Amen.

Egyptian tomato soup with pyramid toast

Egypt is famous for pyramids and spices. May these foods remind us that God kept King Jesus safe in Egypt!

Ingredients
(for 4 bowls of soup)

Time needed 30 mins

- 1 tbsp cooking oil
- 1 onion/brown onion, roughly chopped
- 1 garlic clove, crushed/minced
- 100g/4oz jar red/bell peppers, roughly chopped
- 450g/14.5 oz can chopped/diced tomatoes
- 450ml/15 fl oz chicken or vegetable stock/broth
- ¼ tsp paprika
- ¼ tsp chilli powder (mild probably best for small children!)
- 1 lime, cut into quarters
- 7 slices bread

Equipment

- Large saucepan
- Wooden spoon
- Blender/food processor
- Toaster or grill

Egyptian tomato soup

Traditional Egyptian tomato soup is hot and spicy. Most small children will struggle with the heat, so this recipe is more child-friendly, if less authentic!

1.

Heat the oil in the pan over a medium heat for 1 minute. Then add the onions and garlic, and stir occasionally for 5 minutes or until soft.

2.

Add the peppers, tomatoes and stock/broth to the pan and cook for 10 minutes.

3.

Add the chilli and paprika and cook for 5 more minutes.

4.

Leave the soup to cool a little for 10 minutes. Then blend the soup until smooth.

5.

Pour the soup into bowls and leave until cool enough for your child. Squeeze a piece of lime into each bowl of soup.

6.

Toast the bread. Once the toast is cool enough to handle, stack the slices to make a pyramid. (See drawing to help you.)

While you cook...

• What did the angel tell Joseph?

• Why did Herod hate Jesus?

• What did Mary, Joseph and Jesus have to leave behind?

• Who kept Jesus safe in Egypt?

Note:

If you don't want to make 7 slices of toast, just make one, cut it into triangles and stack them against each other to make a small pyramid.

While you eat...
Why did Mary and Joseph have
to take Jesus to Egypt?

The greatest Christmas present

John 3 v 16

"For God so loved the world that he gave his one and only Son, that whoever believes in him shall not perish but have eternal life." (John 3 v 16)

How much do you think God loves us?

God loves us so much that he wants to give us an amazing present. Can you guess what it might be? It's not a toy. It's not a book. It's not even wrapped up in paper. No, God's present to us is his precious Son, Jesus!

Seasonal gifts

You can make some of these seasonal gifts as Christmas presents, thank you presents or 'just because' presents for your friends, family and neighbours! Put them into a bag or box and attach Jesus' words from John 3 v 16 (see page 48 for labels). Then you can remind them that Jesus is the best present EVER!

Does that sound strange? That God would give us a person as a present? But here's why it's so wonderful. You see, Jesus is the great Rescuer. He can rescue us from living without God and his forgiveness. He died on the cross so that God can forgive us for all the wrong things we have done. How could we not want that?!

Taking God's present means being God's friend. And anyone who says 'yes' to God's present gets to live with God in his perfect home, for ever and ever. Wow! That makes Jesus the best present EVER.

So next time you open a present, remember Jesus. Jesus is the best present EVER!

Pray: Father God, thank you for Jesus, the best present ever. Thank you that because of Jesus, I can be your friend for ever. Help me to love Jesus this Christmas. Amen.

Snowball truffles

Ingredients
(for 20 truffles)

- 150ml/2/3 cup double or heavy cream
- Few drops orange flavouring (optional)
- 150g roughly chopped dark or plain chocolate, or 1 cup dark chocolate chips
- 100g / 1 1/3 cups desiccated or shredded coconut

Equipment

- Small saucepan
- Wooden spoon
- Mixing bowl
- Plate
- Teaspoon
- Baking tray or plate covered in baking paper or parchment

Time needed
15 mins
(plus 3 hrs to set)

1. Heat the cream in the saucepan until it just begins to boil. Add the orange flavouring, if using.

2. Put the chocolate into the bowl. Pour the cream over the chocolate and mix it until all the chocolate melts. Leave the mix on the side to cool and then place it in the fridge for 2-3 hours to set.

3. Tip the coconut onto a plate. Run your clean hands under cold water and don't dry them.

4. Use the teaspoon to take small heaps of mixture and roll them into balls with your hands. Then roll each ball in the coconut so your truffle is covered in snow! Put your snowballs onto the tray or plate.

While you cook...
- Why has God given us a present?
- What is his present to us?
- What does God want us to do with his present?
- Why is Jesus the most wonderful present?

While you eat...

Jesus is the best present EVER. How can you get to know Jesus better?

1.

Sieve the icing sugar into the bowl. Add two teaspoons of egg white, the peppermint and the food colouring, if using. Mix well with the spoon and then with your hands. Add more egg white bit by bit until it all comes together.

2.

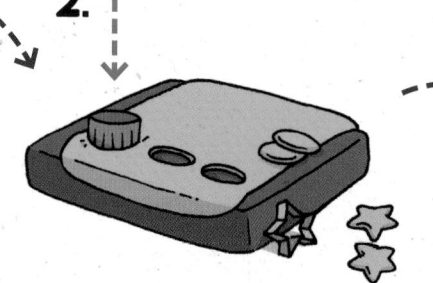

Sprinkle icing sugar lightly onto a clean surface. Then roll out the mixture to about 5mm/¼". Cut out shapes and place them on the trays.

3.

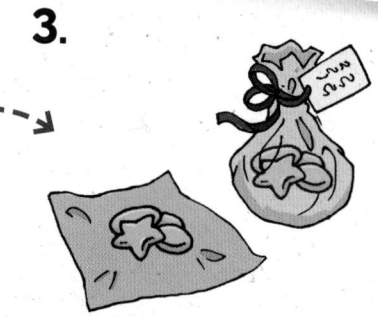

Leave to harden for an hour before putting in a bag or box.

Ingredients
(for 25 shapes)

- 225g/1 ⁴/₅ cups icing sugar/ powdered sugar plus a little extra
- 1 packet of powdered egg white,* reconstituted according to packet instructions
- Few drops peppermint flavouring
- Few drops green food colouring (optional)

Equipment

- Sieve
- Mixing bowl
- Wooden spoon
- Rolling pin
- Small cookie cutters
- 2 baking trays covered in baking paper/parchment

*Safer than using raw eggs

Time needed
30 mins
(plus an hour to harden)

Candy Js

Ingredients
(for 25 shapes)

- 100g/4oz white roll-out icing/rolled fondant
- 100g/4oz red roll-out icing/rolled fondant

Equipment

- Knife
- 2 baking trays covered in baking paper/parchment

Time needed
....
45 mins
(plus 24 hrs to dry out)

1.

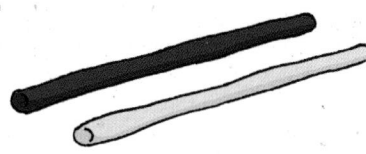

Roll half of the white icing into a very long and very thin sausage (as thin as a pencil) on a clean work surface. Do the same with half of the red icing.

While you cook...
- Why has God given us a present?
- What is his present to us?
- What does God want us to do with his present?
- Why is Jesus the most wonderful present?

2.

Lay the red and white sausages next to each other and twist them together. Then gently roll them together until they are completely smooth.

3.

Cut into 12cm/5" lengths and bend the end to make the "J". Carefully put them onto a baking tray. Repeat with the other halves of the icing. (If you did it in one go, your sausage shapes would be too long for the table!)

4.

Leave them to dry out for 24 hours before putting them in a bag or box.

Note:

"J" is for Jesus: God's gift to us!

45

About the authors

Susie Bentley-Taylor now lives in London, having lived in Oxford for many years. She is married to Pete and they have two precious children: Joshua (4) and Molly (2). She loves Jesus, reading, writing, being outside and cooking (of course!)—both with and without the happy company of her children!

Bekah Moore grew up in South Yorkshire and, after spending many years in Oxford, she is now back north, in Hartlepool. She is married to Nick and they have two sons, Simeon (4) and Francis (2) who, like Bekah, love the beach, food and Jesus. They are part of the church family at All Saints Stranton.

Thank you

A huge thank you to the team at the Good Book Company, especially Alison and André, for turning our idea into a reality, and for all their input along the way.

Thanks to our children Joshua and Molly, Simeon and Francis, who have been enthusiastic participants throughout the whole process! This book is written out of our desire for them to love Jesus all their days, coupled with our love of baking with them! Huge thanks to our husbands, Pete and Nick, for their support, encouragement and wisdom.

And thank you to all those who have been so encouraging about Bake through the Bible. We have been so excited to hear how it has been used to reach so many young children with the good news of the Bible.

Bible-centred resources
for children and families

Play through the Bible

Over 140 play activities to explore the Gospel of Luke with preschoolers.

Bake through the Bible

20 fun cooking activities to explore the Bible story with young children.

The Christmas Promise

A captivating retelling of the Christmas story showing how God kept his promise to send a new King, with superb illustrations by Catalina Echeverri.

Also available:

The Christmas Promise Advent Calendar

The Christmas Promise Colouring and Activity Book

thegoodbook.co.uk/moreforfamilies
thegoodbook.com/moreforfamilies

Downloads

Visit our website for downloads

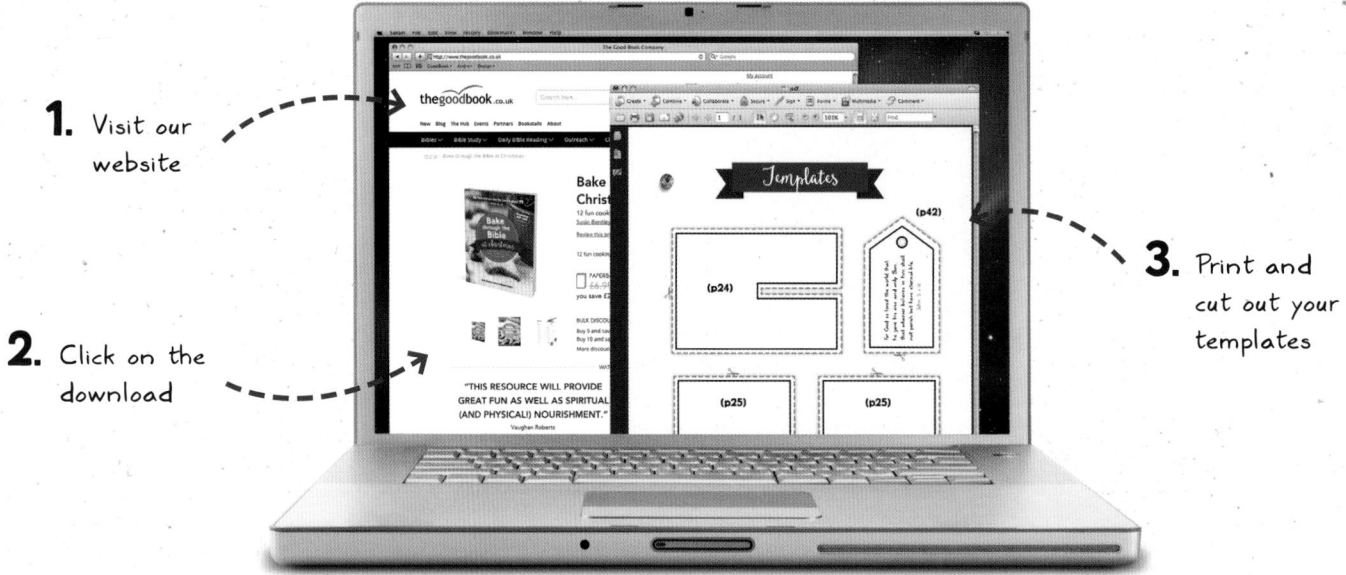

1. Visit our website

2. Click on the download

3. Print and cut out your templates

thegoodbook.co.uk   thegoodbook.com

Templates

(p42)

(p24)

For God so loved the world that he gave his one and only Son, that whoever believes in him shall not perish but have eternal life.

John 3 v 16